*H*EAVEN'S DOOR

The story of a young boy who died and his spirit went up to Heaven, but GOD granted him to return to earth to achieve his goals.

The most spiritual experience being in Heaven

DODI MULINYAWE

xulon PRESS

9-14-17

Dear Dr. Phares

May God bless you and your love ones now and forever.

Love,
Todi

9-14-17

Dear Dr. Chase

Chapter 1

My name is Dodi Mulinyawe.

I was born in the hot island of Luzon, Philippines, about seventy five kilometers from the capital of Manila, in a small town called Alaminos, Laguna. My mother's name was Eulogia and my father was Benito. I only had one sister named Andrea. Our town was very small, I knew most people that lived there. We were very poor, there was no television, no radio, telephone and no running water in our house. I was a very sick boy. When I was two years of age, I developed severe Epilepsy. Each week I would have two attacks, but because my parents were so poor, they couldn't take me to any nearby hospital in the city or to see a doctor in our town. My health problem went on for three years. One time I had a terrible seizure, and my mom thought I was going to die at that particular moment. She then prayed so hard and told GOD, "Father, please spare my son's life, make him well, remove all the sickness from his body. I promise that I will celebrate his birthday every year, and I will always be thankful." When I turned five years old my Epilepsy miraculously disappeared, and I was never given any medicine at all, and yet I was cured. My mother would invite little boys and girls to come to the house, just to celebrate my birthday, and she did all that for many years, until the day she died. I knew what kind of mother she was, she had true faith in GOD that lead to action.

There was a wealthy family in my neighborhood, they had a very big black and white television. My friends and I would watch T.V. but not inside the house, we were not allowed to enter. We had to climb a tree next to the window and that's how we could watch all Western movies. We loved John Wayne very much.

There was a long account of the day of my father's death, which happened when I was five years old, the same year when I recovered from my sickness. How did I know that? Well, I just knew it. According to my mother he just collapsed and suddenly died. But I remembered when I saw my mom crying, I could see the tears in her eyes. My father was gone. I had lots of vivid memories about my father. I was sitting on his lap one night and he told me stories when he was about my age. He told me that his dad was a very honest man in his town and he was always there to help others. I loved my father even though we did not have much time together. He became an alcoholic- perhaps all of his internal organs gave up and he had a heart attack. I cannot remember my dad that much but I knew I had a father. I never had a picture of him. I longed to glimpse a little bit of how he looked. Some folks in my town told me that my father was a good man. He was well respected and most importantly, he was tall and a very handsome man. "Wow, did

I inherit his look somehow?" Maybe, but not his height, I am not that tall, really!!

After a year since the death of my dad my mother re-married. I had never seen this man, I discovered he came from a faraway town. I had a very bad impression the moment I laid my eyes on him. He looked mean and he did not dress well, as if he worked in the mine. I asked myself over and over again, "Would this man accept me?" At first, he was very timid towards me, I just smiled at him but I was nervous as well. Still, I never knew how long my stepdad courted my mother – it was a mystery to me, for years. I have never found out until this day.

I started my grade school at age six, the requirement age was seven, but my mom talked to the teacher and told her I was smart enough. I did not think I would be kicked out later on, I was very excited, indeed. My teacher was so nice. The first month I learned a lot how to memorize

English letters from ABC all the way to Z. We could also sing each English word with harmony. We learned a lot naming all animals in English. I was also very good in mathematics and science.

December had arrived, in our classroom we learned about the spirit of Christmas and when Jesus was born. I also learned that Santa Claus was real. This is the first time I'd ever heard about any of this. All of us were excited when our teacher told us to hang up stockings the night before Christmas. So when Santa comes he would fill the stocking with gifts. I went to bed early, after I hung all my three stockings. I woke up very excited that Christmas day. I went to see what kind of gifts I received from Santa, when I saw the stockings they were all empty. Not even a piece of candy. I was so sad, my tears were rolling down on my cheeks. "Why did Santa ignore me?" I thought. I really believed in him.

The same day all of my friends came to my house to play. They all had their toys given from Santa. I showed them the car I just built made from a flat sardines can. On each side I made two holes and bamboo sticks and corks I made the wheels. I played along with them even though they were making fun of my car. I still didn't understand why Santa did not come to my house. "Did he get lost and he never found my house?" I thought. I guess my mom and my sister did not know who Santa Claus was. I never asked both of them anyhow. I just let it go and I am hoping maybe next Christmas I would be lucky.

Chapter 2

It had been more than a year since my stepdad came into my life. I soon learned that he loved to drink alcohol. He was always drunk, he bothered me so much and I did not want to be near him at all. He would scream at me as if he wanted to hit me. I was so scared of him from day one. He and my mom had leased a farm together. They would plant corn, rice, peanuts, and other kinds of crops. Each year they would harvest and sell the goods to the buyer in town. Some seasons were not good because of bad typhoons and the crops would be destroyed. It would be a big blow to my mom and my stepdad. But one season, I remembered the harvest was almost doubled. My mom and my stepdad were both very happy, they had extra money, but my stepdad didn't give anything to my mother. Come to my surprise, all the money was lost in the gambling house, just in one day. My mom was crying, I started hating this man. From that day I started ignoring him, I never wanted to talk to him, but he did not care at all.

He had a hearing problem. I kept on swearing behind his back, many times he would turn around and asked me what I had just said. I would respond. "Nothing, I hope you have a nice day." I was sure he knew I lied.

The farm was around over an hour and half by foot from our house. We had one horse and a water buffalo. I loved the horse, many times I would ride around the farm during weekends. I would take both animals to the farmland to feed them with green grass. I remembered one Saturday, my stepdad told me not to come home unless the stomach of the two animals were full. I used to sit down under the coconut tree for hours. I wished I had a transistor radio or a book to read, just to kill time.

One night the horse was stolen, my stepdad had money set aside for any ransom, but nobody came forward. We had found out the horse was killed and the meat was sold to a nearby village for consumption. One of our neighbors was the mastermind named Ajax, he was a notorious thief, and he was killed after a few months during another incident. I never knew why he was killed, but I had an idea. Crime really paid for that guy. I was very sad, that horse was my friend. I did miss him a lot. I kept on remembering him for a long time.

My mom worked so hard on the farm. She cultivated and pulled all the bad weeds from between the young crops. She was always under the hot sun every day.

She was always obeying my step-dad. I could feel how much she loved him no matter what happened.

I started to be depressed. I felt no one ever cared for me, I was not as happy as I wanted to be. Many times, I would visit my own dad's grave just to talk to him. I knew he was watching me. The cemetery was only blocks away from our house. I would visit my dad as often as I could at any given time.

During that period, I was very superstitious, I believed in ghosts. In my town most people were saying when a person was gravely ill a bad spirit would come nearby and smelled death. The spirit would turn into a big dog or some kind of animal. It did happen when I came home late at night, I saw a very big dog staring at me. He was near the house of a gravely ill person. I had never seen that dog in my life. He was huge, and tall, he looked scary. I ran so fast. My street was very dark, but I made it home. I slept alone on weekdays because my stepdad and my mom stayed on the farm from Monday to Friday. They had a very tiny bamboo house to sleep in. They came to stay with me on the weekends, so I had two days with them. I wanted to see my mother often, but there was no other way for her to do that. She should and must, be with her loving husband.

Chapter 3

At age seven, I had learned how to cook for myself. I ate lots of rice and corn. I hardly ate meat, (I could not afford it). But I ate lots of vegetables from my mom's garden. Many times I ate white rice with soy sauce and lemon just to have something in my stomach. I knew it was kind of awful but I had no other choice. My childhood was not very good. I had seen lots of abuse. First, my grandpa often beat my aunt (my mom's older sister). I did not really understand why my grandpa did all those things. Nobody ever stopped him. To my knowledge, my grandpa prohibited any guys to see her. She never met any man that she could be friends with. My aunt Julia was beautiful, but I could see on her face the pain and suffering she had endured. Her body was deteriorating, she had long hair touching her shoulders. My grandma used to comb her hair and braided it. Aunt Julia sat mostly by the window all day long, and watched those birds flying and singing outside. She loved butterflies. Aunt Julia often talked and smiled as if someone was there. I kept remembering how sad her life was and it made me cry. She never saw a doctor until my poor aunt Julia died miserably, no one by her side. I felt bad for her. May God bless her soul.!!!

My mother had two more other younger sisters; one was aunt Damasa, and aunt Soledad. My aunt Damasa was not that lucky either. She produced six children, and after the last child she developed lung cancer. To my recollection, my aunt had only seen the doctor once or twice. The doctor's visit will cost more than hundred pesos. Her husband started to neglect her and verbally abusing her. I witnessed all the abuse, because I often played with my cousins when I was at their house.

I didn't remember how long she had suffered with her cancer. Many times she was just laying down on her bamboo bed, and I would buy bread and a soda for her. Sometimes her husband would not come home for days, it was so cruel of him to do that. We found out he had a mistress living on the other side of town, and he fathered three kids. What kind of a man would do awful things like that? He would not bring food for the table, and he would not try to provide money to send my aunt to the hospital. It was a very unfortunate situation, but I was only concerned about my aunt. I could not do anything. She also died alone, similar to Aunt Julia.

Now, my Aunt Soledad was the luckiest one. She had eight children. Her husband was a nice man. Each time I made a visit with my mother, he would pay attention to me and he treated me like his own son. I started to call him Uncle Leon. All of the siblings were becoming successful. One of my cousins seemed to look like me but the oldest son made it big. His name was Felipe. Because he was very tall, charismatic and smart, his business became big. He owned few big trucks, buying millions of coconuts, bananas and other products. He had a big buyer in Manila. He was still single but he was engaged to be married to a girl next door, but I heard he had few more girlfriends, somewhere. He was famous because according to all his friends, he could be mistaken for the guy named Eddie Guttierez, the popular actor in the Philippines. I did envy Felipe and wished I could be successful like him someday. But I was disgusted by him, for the reason that he did not even offer to help his two aunts before they died. They were his mother's sisters, did he think about that? For all the money he had? It was not fair, really. Luckily, the day of Felipe's wedding, my mom and I were invited. We came very early in the morning because my mother offered to help. Then, my cousin and I were playing and we ended up in Felipe's room. On his bed was his wedding outfit; a new black suit, white shirts, pants, socks and new shoes. I wanted to do a little joke just to get even with Felipe by hiding his socks. I made sure I knew where I put them. The time came when he started to dress up, the first thing he looked was his new socks. We all heard him screaming, "Mom!! Where are my socks?" He was so furious. I got nervous, I did not want to admit I was the one who took them. Everyone in the house volunteered to search for the new socks. I did not want them to know it was I that responsible. I just could not admit it, I just couldn't!!!!!!

I was very good at pretending, the socks were never found, but Felipe did not feel good wearing his old socks. He was still mad and couldn't figure out who committed the crime. I never told anyone what I had done. Some years later, my cousin Felipe was killed in a car accident that devastated my aunt Soledad, and the whole family as well. Since then, my aunt Soledad became ill and died. We were all sad. My mom was the only sibling that was left.

I also witnessed how my stepdad abused or molested young girls. They were all my cousins and nieces. One time we had a family gathering, the girls decided to sleep over. One night I could not sleep, there was only a little kerosene light in the corner of the house, I saw my stepdad crawling, headed towards those innocent little girls. I saw him like a giant shadow, a real monster ready to attack. I just covered my face, I did not know what happened next. It was my secret I never told anyone even my mother. I was afraid my stepdad would kill me. Now, I understood why my sister suddenly got married when my stepdad came into our lives. She was just 14 years old. I still remembered what she was wearing, her wedding dress, she was so beautiful. The wedding was so much fun. There were lots of people. I guessed the whole town came, and there were lots of little children as well. I saw a very big pig being roasted. There were lots of food for everyone. My brother-in-law's name was Bartolomew, I did not like him at all, and I still could not believe how Andrea fell in love with that guy. "Why, Andrea, Why?"!!! He did not like me either, I could not care less anyhow. I missed my sister so very much. She did not stay longer with our dear mother. I assumed she made a right decision by getting married. That way she would be safe not being molested by my stepdad. We still had some bonding with each other even though she was older than me.

The verbal abuse by my stepdad continued to grow, he hated me and I hated him. Every time we sat down by the dining table we both looked at each other's eyes hatefully. I told my mom from now on I would prefer eating alone. Whatever was left over, was what I would eat. Since then, I had been eating alone, but I had a cat named Bernie as my companion. He was such a stubborn animal. Every time I started eating my food he would jump and wanted me to feed him right away. One time he purposely grabbed my food. It made me really mad. I got a big brown rice sack and put him inside, I walked for two miles, then I saw a cliff and I just left him there. I saw him running down the hill, I waited for a few more minutes until I took off. I felt bad for what I did. I was so cruel to Bernie. After two days, I started missing him a lot, but I knew I was wrong. To my surprise, he came back seven days after he had been gone. He looked a little thinner. I was happy he came back, but he seemed to change. He was not that aggressive anymore. I guessed, he learned a big lesson. I treated him well and never abused him anymore. We became good friends as well.

Chapter 4

I finally finished my grade school, I was just twelve years old. I was very happy that soon, I would be attending High School. In my country after six years in the elementary school, it will take only four more years to finish High School. If I would be lucky I will start my college at the age of 16 years old. But my stepdad told my mother I wouldn't be attending High School. I would have to work in the farm every day. I objected, I said, "I don't want to be a farmer like you, I have no future". I just wouldn't do it!!! He was going to beat me up, but I warned him that I would retaliate against him. That was my very first time to become aggressive towards him. He was very surprised. Now, he would have to watch me from now on. I never in my life during that period of time, learned to respect him, because he never treated me the way he should have. If he only showed me compassion or took me as his son, then maybe I would call him dad, why not? But nothing happened like that at all. I did not know who was to blame. Was it my fault? I was lost really. I had no one to talk to. I kept everything to myself. I decided to see my sister Andrea, I arrived at her home. I was very sad and upset. By then she already had six children, she had been pregnant almost every year. The first time she had a miscarriage, so I guessed she was very young then. I told her about me not attending school. I asked her if she could help me but her answered was no. She said she and Bartolomew were already having a hard time getting by. I understood her perfectly, I was just finding whatever resources I could find.

My mom finally convinced my stepdad that I should go to high school. I was really happy because my mom

fought very hard for me and my stepdad lost the battle.
I should say that my mother was a very strong woman.

My freshman year I was bullied terribly. I was a very
small guy. I couldn't defend myself. They would push
me behind my back until I fell into the ground. They
called me names like idiot with chicken legs. Many
times I did not want to go to school at all. I just wanted
to stay home, to feel sorry for myself. I almost purchased
a small gun just to scare them. But the bullying stopped,
thank goodness. They were bullying another guy and
they were reported. They were summoned to the office
of the Principal including their parents. They were given
a warning, the next time, they would be suspended for
the whole year. I was relieved that nobody would be bullying me anymore.

During that period of time, I had my eyes on Dory,
she lived in my neighborhood. I really liked her a lot,
but I was shy and scared to let her know how I felt for

her. She had a cousin that I asked for help to deliver my love letters to Dory. It went on for a long time. It was our secret. She cared for me as well, but we could not go out because her mother was very strict. We couldn't even go to the movies or something. Eventually, her mother found out everything. She told Dory to forget about me because my family was very poor and that she would not have a good future with me. When I found that out, I felt so hurt. I didn't understand a poor guy like me was not allowed to love someone. I stopped communicating with Dory. It hurt me so badly because she was my first love. To respect her parents I stayed away from her completely. We were in the same High School. Each time I saw her, I just smiled at her, and nothing else. Later on, she went out with some guy. It took me a very long time to forget her. Meanwhile, there was another girl that I was dreaming about. Unfortunately, she was a daughter of one of the richest men in my town. I sent a message through her friend to tell her I had a crush on her. We had met before in one of the gatherings in the Plaza. I was sure she liked me as well. But one of my friends advised me, I should not even try to court her because if her father found out, he would hire someone to beat me up. Her father only welcomed the rich guys to meet his daughter. Otherwise, it would not be possible for me to have a shot. I guessed, I was born that way, always unlucky and unfortunate, in many different ways.

Near my senior year in high school, I had a beautiful dream. I would never forget every event that happened. I died and my spirit immediately flew straight up to heaven. I could feel the breeze. I traveled for a while, then finally reached the front gate. Saint Peter was waiting for me. He said "Come in young man, I will take you to "HEAVEN'S DOOR." We both walked a little bit up on the stairs. There, it was a huge "HEAVEN'S DOOR". From the left the Father was standing, and to the right was his son Jesus Christ. They both looked alike, with beautiful white robes. Their images were so bright like white lights as if they did not have human flesh. Their faces were incredibly spiritual and I looked up again and I asked the Father, "Father, why did you take my life? I have not done anything, I want to help my mom and my sister, and all the people I love, please send me back to earth." "After I have finished all my good accomplishments, then you can take my life back." Then the Father replied, "Son, I will send you back to earth as you wish, you are going to have a long journey in life, you will find whatever you'll be looking for, go on my son. You must take the right road and never turn back", I suddenly moved my head toward Jesus, he smiled at me, I felt so good and I was very touched. I could not believe that moment I was standing there with the Heavenly Father and His son Jesus Christ. Everything around me was a white silky fog, totally incredible. I thanked the Father for sending me back. I waved them goodbye. Then suddenly, I felt my spirit was flying down back to earth. I woke up feeling tired. I knew in my heart that I really died. I told my mother about my dream. I wasn't sure if she was excited or not. She was just stunned and confused. I then asked her why it happened to me. Was my dream for real? Since then I kept my dream a secret. I was very afraid no one would ever believe me. But from time to time, I would ask people if they ever dreamed of God and Jesus. I don't remember anyone who ever told me they did.

When I was still a very young boy, I heard one story from an old man in our town. The story occurred in Jerusalem long, long, time ago, this is what he related to me. In the Promised Land, there was a small village where people young and old preparing themselves for something very special. The rumor spread to every corner of the village, that Jesus Christ would soon be visiting the place the next day. The following morning everyone was excited, they were all busy and getting ready for the spectacular event. There was a woman who was living alone, she had a small house with two little rooms. She started cleaning and decorating her house. The extra room, there was a bed, she put a clean sheet, new blanket and pillow cases. She made sure everything looked good. In her kitchen, she had a special bottle of drinking water. She cooked a special recipe and she baked lots of wheat bread. She made sure that when Jesus comes everything would be ready.

It was almost noon time, there was a knock on her door. She hurriedly opened, it was a small boy, and he said to her, "Lady, I am very thirsty, can you please give me a glass of water." She responded madly!!! "I am sorry the water that I have is only for Jesus, try to ask the people next door, maybe they can assist you." The boy left, he was very disappointed. The woman continued working. After an hour there was another knocked on her door. She rapidly opened, it was a man, his clothes looked dirty and his hair was not neatly combed. The man said,

"Lady, I am so hungry, can you please spare me a little bit of your food, even a piece of bread would be heaven for me." The lady responded angrily, "No, the food I have prepared is only for Jesus, maybe you can ask next door, for sure they can provide food for you." The man was so disappointed as well. He walked towards the next door. It was almost ten o'clock in the evening, the lady was still waiting for Jesus to come. Suddenly, another knock on her door, this time she was so excited, indeed. She then opened the door assuming it was Jesus, but it was an old man, he looked very tired and restless. He said, "Lady, I walked many miles, I have no place to sleep for the night, can you spare me a room so I can rest." Now the lady was really upset. It was already late at night and she was ready to go to bed herself. She told the man, "I only have one room available but I am reserving it for Jesus, He will be here any minute now. You can check next door. Maybe they will provide a room for you." The man walked away looking very sad.

She sat down on a big chair closer to the door. She was tired, and right after, she fell asleep. Eventually, she had a dream that night. Jesus came to her. The lady said, "Jesus, I was waiting for you almost the whole day, why did you not come to visit Me.?" Jesus then replied with a smile, "Lady, I came to you three times but you refused me." When the lady woke up, she was so ashamed of herself, she could not forgive herself for what she had done. From that moment in time, she changed and became more giving and more caring to others. I often thought about this story because there was a strong message to it. We can show our love to God by all means. To open our hearts to others who are in need. Could it be similar to my own dream?

Chapter 5

Two years passed, my dream always fresh in my mind. It seemed I dreamt it the night before, that fresh!!

I finally graduated from high school. I had gained weight and I had grown a little taller. Off course, I had to thank my stepdad and my poor mother as well for their support they had given me. My stepdad never changed. He was still drinking heavily. Now he is more than a bad alcoholic person. He was still a gambler. He never got ahead in his life. My mother had been a "martyr" I was thinking on what to do about her.

One day my stepdad came home very drunk. Again he lost his money in the gambling house, as usual. That moment in time I saw him beating my mother. I was so mad, I needed to find a weapon, a knife or something. Suddenly, I found a big machete. My mom went out screaming. She was petrified. People in the neighborhood came into the streets, and my stepdad ran outside. I followed him, then he fell down on the ground. From there, I was ready to cut his head off. People on the street were shouting, "Go, go, and cut his head off!!!" They wanted to see some action, like in the movies. My blood was boiling, I told those people to get out or else I would kill them too. I held the machete really high, ready to harm my stepdad. Suddenly, there was a man behind me who grabbed my arm and said, "Young man, don't do it, you are going to spend your life in jail." I replied, "I don't care anymore, my life is over, I just want to kill him." The man was still holding my arm. I cooled down a little bit, until I released the weapon from my right arm and gave it to him. He really saved my life as well as my stepdad's. After that I have never seen that man again. He was like an angel who came to the rescue.

That afternoon I went to the cemetery to visit my dad. I said, "Dad, I want to get out of this town, I don't know where, but I will take my mother with me." I wiped the tears coming out from my eyes. "Goodbye dad, please look after me and mom." That night, I sat down with my mother very seriously, I said, "Mom, let's run away, just you and me, you have no more future with your husband,"... "I promise to support you for the rest of your life. We will make it"... "You suffered too much, and don't you think you deserve a change in your life?" But my mother said no. I knew she would never leave her husband. I was determined to leave that night, and I did. My mom was crying until I said goodbye. I just took some of my old clothes. I put them in one old brown paper bag. I told my mother, I did not know where I'll be. I must find a right road to take. I hugged my mother very tightly – I told her I would let her know wherever I landed.

It was almost dark, I was walking towards the main road but I still did not know where to go. I saw the bus coming, I waved to stop. The first city would be San Pablo. I had to think who the first person I must see and asked for help.

- First, I landed in a radio station. My friend Rick worked there as one of the announcers. He was also a dance instructor in my High School, where I participated in a dance school competition. It's funny, when I was growing up I always kept the names of the people I met (good ones) I must remember also where they lived and where they worked. I went inside the station, I saw Rick waving through the glass window. He made a signal to me. He would come out in ten minutes. I waited and sat down on a big sofa. There was a woman that really dressed up. She was pretty, and I was thinking maybe she was Rick's friend, but she was also worked there. Rick finally came out and I started to talk...

I told Rick I ran away from home and that I needed a place to stay for a night or two. He felt bad and told me there was no problem. He would let me sleep on the sofa in the lobby. I was so glad, I could not believe that I was having good luck, so far. He gave me money to buy some food at the Hot Dog stand next to the building. I did not want to accept it, but he insisted. I did spend two nights there, until I decided where to go next. I said goodbye to Rick, I thanked him for his kindness, then I went to the bus station, I sat there for a while, until I decided where I was supposed to go. "Maybe I should go to Los Banos", my first thought. I knew a friend there whom I met way back in one of my school events. I traveled for one and a half hours until I reached my destination. A few blocks from the bus stop I finally found Resty's home. He was outside the house seemed like he was waiting for someone. He was surprised to see me! I told him I wanted to speak with him privately. We went to the basement of the house, he asked me what was in the brown bag, and I could not tell him right away. Then I told him my situation, that I needed a place to stay for the time being, and maybe he could ask his parents to let me stay in their house. He talked to them and the answer was definitely, yes!!

The mother said, since I was a friend of her son, they would be delighted to help me in any way they could.

I was very happy. Silently I thanked God. The family had a little store in the market. Their business was nice. They sold all kinds of sweets, cakes, noodles, etc. They prepared the goods the night before. Then early in the morning they start selling. Since I knew how to work hard, I started helping them from day one. The family was so glad they didn't have to tell me what to do.

The market was not that big. My first day was kind of interesting. I was helping customers but I noticed those young girls from the nearby school kept coming to buy and most of them were always smiling at me. The next day more and more girls were coming to buy. We were always sold out. One old lady nearby said, those girls came just to see me. I was flattered. I was confused what those girls saw in me. At that time my hair was very curly, my nose was a little sharp. I also had a dark skin, I just did not understand why they liked me. I didn't feel I was different, I thought I was ugly. Well, at least I felt special in the eyes of those young girls. Maybe I should become a movie star?? I guessed not.

Way back during my high school years, one of the girls in my class sent my picture to the magazine publication for joining Mr. and Miss Teenager in the Philippines.

I thought it was a prank, but the publication sent me a letter from Manila for me to come for an interview. From there I became one of the candidates. There were lots of fan mails, I had received. Since I didn't have enough money to buy all those magazines to get the ballots, I didn't have a big chance of winning, but I knew it was all the money involved, because I needed to buy thousands of magazines to cut the ballots in order for me to cast all the points, but I was glad for the experience. Meeting some of the Filipino stars. I did meet my favorite actors named Gloria Romero and Eddie Mesa. It was a great moment for me. I think at one time my picture was on the back cover of one of the magazines, full page. Most people in my town were happy for me. Some of them were not. But I didn't care a bit.

Chapter 6

Now back to my new life. The family really loved me. I was not lazy. I did most of the hard work. Besides cooking I had to chop wood every afternoon. The house was on the side of the highway. Different types of buses and jeepneys, would come and go. The people walked by. Every time I chopped wood at 4:00p.m. There were two Americans wearing white short sleeves and ties. I didn't know who they were, but each time they passed by they would smile at me and say hello. I then said Hi back. After two weeks, they finally stopped and introduced themselves to me. First the guy said, "Hi I am Elder Richard Parkinson and this is my companion Elder Ronald Feik," "We are the missionaries from the

Mormon Church". I replied, "I am not familiar with your church, this is the very first time I heard about it." "Do you want to know more?" Elder Parkinson asked, I said, "Of course I am interested to know more." The next day they handed me the Book of Mormon. My problem was I didn't want the family to know I was involved with the missionaries. What I didn't know they were all watching by the window, when I was talking with the missionaries. That same day, the mother told me to stay away from them. They were very strong Catholic. She told me I had to stay away from the Mormons. But I was very interested to know more about the Mormon Church. I felt I was capable enough to make my own decision.

I felt that I had to try everything that came to me, since I was alone and far from my own family, I wanted a fresh start. I wanted to be positive in all aspect of my life. I started reading the Book of Mormon. It was my first time to read that kind of book. I have learned so much about it. I was very happy about the contents of the book. I had to read twice to understand it. When I was a Catholic, I had never received any books to read about the gospel. I didn't even have a Bible. I was not really happy being a Catholic. I seldom went to church. I didn't like the priests at all, because I and my friend were molested when we were kids. We both could not tell anyone even to the police because no one would believe us. Back then, people in my country regarded priests second to God. Also, most people who went to Catholic Church were mostly rich people .They would parade on the streets wearing their fancy clothes and jewelry, just to attend the church. For the poor people it would be a different way to go out. Most of them could not afford to buy new clothes to wear to attend the church. I did not like what was going on in my town but everybody had to dance with the music. If you are poor your are poor, and if you are rich, you are rich. After two weeks, the two Elders came to me and asked me if I had finished reading the Book of Mormon. I happily said "yes".

Now, I was ready to be baptized after lots of discussions with the Elders. I was under age so the two Elders and I had to travel to my hometown to ask my mother's permission, in order for me to be baptized. It was my very first time to come home since I ran away. We arrived in my home town, before we reached the house, people on the streets were all watching, wondering why I was with the two white men. They were all very curious, but no one dared to ask me. They were some young kids who were following us all the way till we reached the house. The Elders met my mom. She didn't know how to speak English, and I needed to translate everything to her. I told my mom not to worry about me because I was in good hands. I had a chance to tell her where I was and whom I was staying with. I told her the family I was staying with were treating me so well. The Elders explained to my mother the purpose of our trip. My mother told him it was okay whatever my decision would be, then it was fine for her. It was a very hot afternoon. I saw a little coconut tree, I climbed and picked some young coconuts for the two Elders to have some refreshments. They loved it, especially the coconut juice. I still couldn't believe that I could climb a coconut tree. Maybe it was not me who climbed the tree.

I did not see my stepdad. Maybe he was in the gambling house at that time. We could not stay longer. I was sure there would be some rumors on why I came with the Elders, the kids who followed us heard everything, so from the time we left until the next morning, it would be a big news in my town. It was a very happy goodbye, for me and my mom. It was very different from the first time I left her, and there were no tears anymore. She was happy and I could see the smile on her face. On the street, some people were still waiting till we came out. I just waved goodbye to all of them, not saying anything. I would let them worry, but I was sure everyone would come to see my mother to ask her what was going on. It was up to my mom whatever she told those curious people. It was fine with me. We took off, back to Los Banos. I was sure we would be home late after another long trip. On the bus, I was sitting next to Elder Parkinson. I told him that I would be staying with the family for as short time till I found my own place. He said they were looking for someone to help them and to take care of the chapel. He offered me the job as their houseboy. I did not hesitate, I said yes right away!! I told him I had to find a way on how I would tell the family, all those things that were happening to me. I would have to figure it out.

Chapter 7

Now, it was my time to be baptized to the LDS Church. The Elders told me to meet them in the place where the church held baptisms. I knew the place so I arrived there in time. I saw few people. Perhaps they were converts by the Elders. I was happy but a little nervous. That weekend I became a member. I was thinking on how I would adjust myself for my new religion I just joined. But I knew it would be a very interesting journey. My problem was, how I was going to tell the family. That night, I sat down with all of them. I couldn't start right away, my heart was beating very fast. Then I said, "Mom, I joined the Mormon Church and I am now a member. I hope you are not mad at me, for not telling you earlier." I thought she would tell me to get out from the house right away, but I was wrong. She said to me, "Is that what you really want" I then replied respectfully, "Yes mom, it was my big decision and I am happy about it, the Elders also offered me a job to work for them." The mother said, "We love you son, and we will all be very sad when you go. If you change your mind, we will help you go to college." I said sadly, "I do appreciate it very much and for everything you all have done for me." I added, "I want to do it on my own, that way I can prove it to myself that I can make it no matter what happens." That night, I left the family, they were all very sad to see me leave especially the mother. I would never forget them, and my friend Resty. They were all part of my journey.

I finally moved in with the Elders. The church was renting the bottom section of the big house. We had the chapel there with fifty chairs. We had one electric organ. There was a big room attached, two big beds for the missionaries and a big sofa for me to sleep. My first day the Elders gave me a to do list. I had no problem following it. They gave me a little allowance for that week and I decided to save it.

My first day I had to wash their clothes. Since we didn't have a washing machine I had to do with my two hands. Each day the Elders needed to change their white shirts three times a day because of the humidity and dust. They sweat a lot. They both have long pants I had a hard time cleaning them. Ring around the collar, that's my problem. But I remembered what my mother showed me, the ring around the collar I had to put lemon and salt, lay the shirt under the sun for about an hour or so, then after that, wash it again with the detergent soap and rinse the shirt well. It did work. "Thank you mother". I still remembered when I used to sit next to her, just to learn everything what she was doing. All the golden rules with which my own mother had blessed me. I always carried them with me.

Our chapel was in the middle of a subdivision compound. Most people there were rich. Many times they looked down on me especially when I was doing or washing the clothes outside the house. There was no space to do the laundry inside the house, so I used the only faucet outside. There was no single soul ever came to say hello. They were just staring at me. I was not ashamed by what I was doing. I just ignored whatever their critics about me. I didn't pay attention to them. There was an old lady living above us, she was the caretaker of the property. We became friends. She talked like a cat but I always avoided laughing at her. Every time I talked to the missionaries I imitated her, they both laughed many times.

It was a good thing I knew how to cook so I tried to feed them with my own recipes. I went to the market one time and bought some fresh shrimps. I prepared it, so it was very tasty and they both liked it. I mixed the shrimps with coconut milk and some fresh ginger. Then I made some white steam rice. I invented very good drinks for the Elders. I would cut one cantaloupe, shred the fruit, mixed with condensed milk and some ice. Refrigerate for an hour or so, "wooo" a perfect drink. They both liked it very much. I took good care of the Elders. They never complained about my work. I was happy everything was working out well for all of us.

I did enjoy helping the missionaries. The members in my ward were so nice to me as well. Brother Abao used to cut Elder Parkinson's hair and he did mine too. Above Elder Parkinson's bed, he had a motto written on a white paper with blue ink, it was posted on the wall. It said, "IF YOU FAIL TO PREPARE, PREPARE TO FAIL". I kept those words in my mind right away, and I really made sure that everything I did had no failures, and it helped a lot for me in everyday life. The Elders always played tricks on me. One time I was so tired, I fell asleep on the sofa. I didn't know how long I was asleep. I felt the electric fan was hitting my face.

Suddenly, I opened my eyes, I asked myself why my body was white from head to toe? I stood up, facing the mirror, then I screamed so loud! I looked scary with my curly white hair. I looked like a zombie. I guessed, they wasted the whole plastic bottle of the baby powder to spread all over my body. I went out of the room. There were the two Elders laughing so hard! I guessed they saw everything, all of my reactions upon seeing myself in the mirror. Elder Feik almost fell down by laughing so hard. I was glad he didn't have a heart attack or something. I didn't know whether I should laugh or cry. But I did laugh as well, it was fun for them. It was not the last time they pulled a trick on me. The second time was terrible. One night they came home around 9:30 p.m., Elder Feik came to me and said Elder Parkinson was very very sick and throwing up lots of blood. This was April the first. I saw Elder Parkinson covering up his mouth with both his hands, and on his knees. I then panicked, I wanted to call an ambulance but we didn't have a phone. I kept pacing and pacing around the house. I didn't know what to do, somehow I took one suitcase and filled up with Elder Parkinson's clothes, I didn't know why I was doing that, then I was running outside to go to one member's house who owned a jeep, so we could take Elder Parkinson to the hospital, immediately. I was going crazy at that time, I didn't want any bad thing to happen to Elder Parkinson. I was really worried, and suddenly, I saw both of them together in one corner laughing so hard! I said, "What is going on here fellows? Explain to me!" I was a little mad already but they never stopped laughing. Then one Elder said, "You know April 1 in America is April fool's day and today is the first of April, so we have to fool you!" I said, "Oh man, I wish I knew". I was still mad and I did a silent treatment to them for two days. Then after that, we all made up and we started laughing once again. I just couldn't get mad at these two men. All I had to do was to laugh with them each time they tricked me. I loved them to death. The members also loved the two Elders and they enjoyed the examples that the Elders were showing them. Somehow I became close to Elder Parkinson. We both never had a brother and we both have a sister about the same age. I made a comment that maybe we were brothers in the spirit world and I was wrongly sent to the Philippines. He started to laugh. He was truly a nice friend and a brother to me. I didn't know he even sent a letter to his mother and told her how nice I was to him and that I was a very honest guy. I respected him so much, he became my mentor. He kept on advising me and telling me to have faith in GOD, and things would be brighter for me anytime soon. I took all his good advice and I told him I would do the best of my abilities to be good and to believe in myself. He really felt bad and he thought my life story was so tragic, and I deserved a happy ending. I did amaze him the way I handled everything. Sometimes he shared with me his life story but compared to mine, his story was full of good things, very few heartaches and disappointments.

Chapter 8

One day we received the bad news that Elder Parkinson would be assigned to the island of Cebu to continue his mission there. The members and I signed a petition and sent it to the mission President asking that Elder Parkinson be allowed to continue his mission service where he was for another six months. But our request was denied. Now we had to face the reality that Elder Parkinson was finally leaving us. The day before his departure we decided to give him a farewell party. We all contributed and cooked lots of food. We decorated the chapel as well. Everyone was there including little children. Brother Abao made a speech thanking Elder Parkinson. I didn't say anything because I was very sad during that particular moment. We started eating all the food that we had prepared. The Elders seemed to like the Filipino food very much. Elder Feik said, "You guys are going to make me fat". (He was already a little heavy). We all wanted to have a good time and tried not to be sad. At the end of the party I asked someone to play the organ, the song we chose from the Hymn book was "GOD BE WITH YOU TILL WE MEET AGAIN." This time we were all crying, I saw most of them wiping their tears away. Then we all said goodbye to Elder Parkinson, he was sad as well. The next day I wasn't sure who came to pick him up, I guessed, he would be in a mission home for a day till he was sent to his next mission. The night before he left, he talked to me that he was going to refer me to brother Pambid in the Manila Branch. He had a friend who owned a business in the city, and maybe I could work there. It was nice of him to spend his time thinking about me and making my life much brighter. It was hard for me to see him leave but there was nothing I could do, but to accept that he was gone. I would see him again for sure, in the near future.

Chapter 9

After a week I went to Manila to meet Brother Pambid. He then called his friend and discussed about me getting a job in the office. I then proceeded to have an interview. Mr. Alcantara was the man who gave me the one hour interview. It went well, I answered each question he had asked me. I admit, I was so nervous but I was hired immediately. He told me how much my salary was, it was not that much but I agreed to take the job. I asked myself again, "Why is everything working out so perfectly?" I asked the manager to give me a week because I had other personal business to take care. He then agreed, I would be reporting to work after a week. I was so happy, really.

I needed to find someone to take my place helping the missionaries. The new Elder came, the replacement for Elder Parkinson. Elder Feik would have another three months before his next assignment. I found someone to take my place. I really hope that guy would stay to help the two Elders. It would be a disaster if he decided to quit. But there were no problems at all. The Elders were happy and contented.

The following weekend I took the bus heading to Manila. I landed in a city called Paco. I knew a guy there named Rolly. He was working in the bank as a manager of one of the departments. He was leasing a big house and he was renting few of the rooms. I met his aunt. She showed me the place, and I had to share the room with another person. She told me I had to furnish my own bed but I could not afford so I slept on the hard floor. All I needed was a mat, a sheet and most importantly, a mosquito net. In the Philippines we had lots of different types of mosquitos, so we all needed some protections from those little vampires. I called Rolly at the bank and told him I would like to be one of his tenants. I had no choice because the following Monday I had to start my new job. I was also offered to have my room and board included with my monthly rent. The meals would be breakfast and dinner, and at least I did not have to cook. I would just eat my lunch at work. The amount was not too bad, I would be able to afford all the expenses from my salary I would receive. It worked just fine.

There were eight people in the compound but there was only one bathroom for all of us. I had to wake up at four thirty every morning from Monday to Friday so that I was the first one to use the bathroom. My roommate's name was Romy. He also worked in the bank. He was engaged ready to be married. He had a guitar, one night he sang a song to me. He sounded terrible and I pretended I liked it. He was very nice to me. He was wondering why I was sleeping on the floor. I told him I was saving my money for future expenses. He told me I could get my bed on credit but I decided not to do that. I had been sleeping on the floor since the day I was born, so it was not a big problem at all.

That following Monday was my first day at work. I was very nervous, indeed. When I arrived, the first thing I did was to introduce myself to everybody. We had twenty staff including myself. They all had their own positions and responsibilities. I had my own little desk and a typewriter. My boss told me all my duties, I would be typing the company's checks, letters, depositing funds to the bank, filling documents and answering some phone calls, if it was necessary. We had our receptionist but I had to watch the phone calls when she was out of the building. I was glad I took a typing class when I was in High School. It was really important to learn many different things in life because someday we could use all the knowledge we accumulated in our brains. In a case like mine, I was amazed, it did not hurt me going through all the things I needed to know. It was my very first time working in the office, so everything was very exciting. The people in the office were incredible. They all treated me nice as if I knew them for a long time. I noticed that wherever I went people seemed to like me and truly appreciated me. I felt I had a gift in me.

My company's name was Sierra Madre Mining Company, owned by a very rich Chinese business man. We had a big mining location in Davao, the other island called Visaya. During that time the company found traces of gold and silver in one area of the mountain. There were lots of rich Chinese people who came to us to invest. Our company was already listed in the Stock Exchange in Manila, and the shares were still very low but once our company really started mining gold, then the stocks would definitely goes high. Our building was located in the heart of Escolta, still in Manila. Many big corporations were there, they owned big buildings and businesses. Our area was what I called, the place of the Rich and Famous. I had seen politicians, celebrities and foreigners, as well. One time my boss asked me to pick up his lunch he ordered in one of the famous restaurants. He knew the owner there. They were lots of famous people, mostly movie stars. I had seen them only on T.V. or magazines and there I was, mingling with the stars. I pretended I was not paying attention to them, though they could see me dressed terribly. When I came back to the office I didn't tell anyone who I saw in the restaurant. It was already my lunch break, I went downstairs to buy my sandwich. I had to watch my budget, otherwise I would be in trouble the way I handled my money. I still wanted to give some money to my mother every month.

I had an hour lunch. I went for a walk along the Boulevard. I also stopped in one big department store. I was shocked when I saw all the prices on all the items. The shirt I wanted cost almost two weeks of my paycheck. It was not my store, I have to go where poor people shop, and I did that. Poor people like myself dress simple and very casual.

Chapter 10

From my boarding house to work I would spend an hour and a half one way, by transit bus. If I was lucky, and if there was no traffic, then I could arrive in the office on time or even earlier than eight in the morning. The traffic always bumper to bumper. There were so many cars, buses and jeepneys, so I had to get used to it. Air pollution started to get worse but there was nothing that I could do. I still loved to live in the province. There was no smog, and all the coconut and banana trees were all over the place. Here in the city, they were so many different people from all over the country. Quiapo was the center of Manila. There was a big Catholic Church there that displayed Jesus of Nazareth, colored in black. Lots of catholic people go there to kiss Jesus's hand and to light candles. Different street vendors, they were selling all kinds of things like toys, dried peanuts, and all kinds of fresh fruits. Each vendor was required to pay a daily fee, as all the money being collected would be handed to the leader of the Mafia Gang, some policemen were also part of the daily activities, and they made extra money for themselves.

There were so much corruptions in my country, but that was part of everybody's life. Most people who worked for the government were all related to the President of the Philippines, and also related to his wife Imelda Marcos. One time I joined a field trip for one day. I took a day off that Friday. We went to Ilocos Norte, the place where President Ferdinand Marcos was born. We were doing a survey to find out what kind of job most people in that Province were doing. The group was funded by one of the Non Profit Organizations and I was one of the volunteers to sign up. Then I had a chance to have a conversation with two middle age men who were playing cards and drinking San Miguel Beer (the only beer being sold in the country). The company was owned by a Filipino millionaire, not even imported beer was allowed to sell in my country. I started my conversation. It was already almost noon time. I asked one of the men and I said, "So, may I ask where you work?" He then answered, "I worked for the government, and I do nothing." I replied, "What do you mean you do nothing, you should be at work right now." The other man said the same thing. I just found out that most of the people there were on Government payroll as if they were collecting pensions. Marcos was in power more than 25 years and he controlled everything. Those people were receiving pay checks and they were not required to work. It made me sick to my stomach. Luckily, we came home safe otherwise we could had been arrested for what we were doing. During that time there was already the

MARSHALL LAW. Many people had vanished with no trace.

If a person became educated, he or she would have a hard time finding a job, if there was no connection to the higher authority. One thing that I was very proud of was, we focused on education. The country had so many professionals or educators, doctors, lawyers, nurses and school teachers. Most poor parents tried very hard to have their children to be educated and to have their career no matter what it took. It was the only investments they could give to their children. I wanted to be a school teacher, but the pay was so little. Since that time, there were so many nurses and doctors who went abroad to seek for more opportunities to make money. Lots of them were so successful, and they were able to help their own families when they sent U.S. dollars back home. More and more people wanted to go abroad. I myself, thought about it, but I had to wait. I still did not know what I was going to do because at that time I was not yet a professional.

There was no Government assistance to help the poor, everywhere throughout the country. If any member of the family got sick, liked heart attack or something, the hospital required to show them the bank book. When there's not enough money in the account, the patient would be sent home to die. NO MONEY, NO SERVICE. It was awful...I remembered when my mother passed away, the nurse told us that if we were not there, the Body Snatcher would pick up my mom's body to take to a Funeral home of their choice. Then we would be required to pay them with enormous amount of money, when we claim the body, otherwise we would not be able to get my mom's body out. That kind of activities were also run by big corrupt officials. Could you blame me why I hate my own country?

Chapter 11

I was enjoying my job. I didn't have good salary but it helped me to pay my rent and to buy new clothes. I needed to wear nice clothes, because I worked in the office. I was still waiting for my next pay day so I could buy my new shoes. Too bad, I was still using my very old shoes. After I received my first pay check, I made a copy so I could hang on the wall at my boarding house. I made new friends at work and at the bank we were dealing with. I was so lucky to meet business people who inspired me, I was wishing and praying someday I would be like them. I was only a High School graduate but I always thought of how I could improve myself.

I still remember what my grandpa told me. When someone dream about the future make sure to dream big. Take advantage, it is only a dream and maybe it will happen. I had been doing that ever since.

During that period I often visited my mother in my old town. I also made peace with my stepdad. I told my mother that I was really enjoying my life in a big city. She did not have to worry about me, once again. Each time I came to visit I made sure I had something for mom and my stepdad. I did not hate him anymore.

Chapter 12

I was very active in the church. I got involved with home teaching. Sometimes I was asked to teach Sunday school with the kids of my age. My bishop was a nice man. I got along with him very well. I began to realize that I was becoming a better person. That year was our youth conference. It was held in Los Banos, the town where I started becoming an LDS. I could not believe how many young men and young women were there. I met most of them. We all enjoyed the time we spent together during the conference. I learned so much and I would never forget those guys that I met. It was one of the most beautiful experiences of my life. I was so glad most of the young members enjoyed my company, most of them became my friends as well. I made sure I would not forget their names, and I would be happy to meet them again.

Elder Richard Parkinson was still in Cebu. I had never heard from him since he left Los Banos. I did not know what was going on with him but later I found that he was doing alright where he was. I was anxious to see him again. I had so many good things to share with him, I was sure he would be excited to know more about all the progress I made. I could not wait to meet him face to face, once again.

Six months had passed, I heard Elder Parkinson was one of the candidates to become assistant to President Rose, he was our mission President at that time. There were few of the Elders to be chosen, I told myself, "I am pretty sure Elder Parkinson will be chosen." There was another Elder who was very smart, but he looked like a model of men's clothes magazine, I did not feel he would be the one. I met him many times, he seemed to be nice, but he was very good looking, it might hurt him. To my surprise, Elder Parkinson was chosen. (By the way, Elder Parkinson was good looking too). That time he came back from Cebu and started his new position. I called to congratulate him, he was happy to hear my voice. Now, I would spend more time on seeing him because the Mission House was very near to Manila Branch, where I belonged. I saw him walking side by side with the mission President mostly on Sundays, all the Mission Presidency held their meetings at our branch, so I met the Elder often.

One incident like at 1:00 p.m. I was at work when suddenly, a big earthquake hit the city, it was so strong, the building was swaying, and we all hid under the desks. When it was all over I called Elder Parkinson at the Mission Home to find out if he was alright. Thank goodness, he was okay. He told me he was pretty shaky as where the rest of the people in the building. I was always worried about him.

Chapter 13

Being a member of the LDS church had changed my whole life. I became a more caring person and I often asked the Lord to bless everyone, especially my family and friends. I knew that someday I would be able to better myself but I must take the right road and to climb the stairs one step at a time. One weekend, I was with some youth in the church. After the church meetings we were all discussing what we were going to do in the future. One of the guys suggested we should go to college in Hawaii. I said, "Don't discuss that because it's impossible for me to study abroad, let's talk about something else". The next week I heard lots of the youth members were considering to study in Hawaii. Some of them already had applications. I was not really interested but one of my friends persuaded me to fill out the application. I said I would do it for fun. I finally filled it out along with other requirements. The next day I sent the application in the mail. I didn't expect for any response from the school. But to my surprise, I was the first one to receive the letter of acceptance. The next time I met my friends, I showed them the letter I just received from BYU Hawaii Campus. They could not believe it because I was the one who was not interested, and then I was the very first one to get accepted. To me it was a miracle. I could not believe it either. Two weeks later everybody got their letters of acceptance from the University.

Now, most of the youth were busy getting their paper work done. There were rumors on who was going and who wasn't, I was one that was not going. I knew it was impossible for me to proceed, so I just kept quiet and I never discussed it with anybody, although I wished I could go. Most of the members found out about my situation. One American family sent me a message to come to see them. I was very worried on why the family wanted to see me. "Did I do something wrong?" I couldn't think of anything I did. I finally met them in their house. I was told to have a seat, and I did so, nervously. Mr. Broadbent was the head of the family. He was one of the scientists stationed in the Philippines to study about rice in the country. I was the first one to speak, and I said, "Brother Broadbent, may I ask you why you wanted to see me?" He responded, "Well, me and my family found out you were not going to BYU- Hawaii to attend college there. We knew the reason why. You are such a nice guy and we are going to help you to pay your plane ticket." I was very shocked and speechless. I couldn't believe what I was hearing. I had to pinch my arm to see if I was dreaming. It was real, I didn't know how to thank them. I accepted the offer and I almost broke down to tears, but I held everything inside. I knew my eyes were watery. They also told me not to worry paying them back, it was their gift to me, and I tried not to be emotional. They were such a nice family, I guessed they were watching me since I joined the church and they knew what kind of a person I was. I felt I had impressed them a great deal. I didn't tell anyone about the plane ticket. It had been my secret for a long time.

Chapter 14

With all the excitement I was having, I started working on my papers to send to BYU-Hawaii. I also told all of my friends that I was ready to apply. No one ever questioned me about anything. I completed all the necessary requirements. In two weeks' time I received all the proper documents I needed for the U.S. embassy in Manila. I needed to produce different types of documents. There were some members who helped me to give copies of the titles of their homes, required by the U.S. Embassy. Another member helped me to give an affidavit of support. They were so many requirements I needed to complete. But I made it all possible.

Most of my friends were already ahead of me. Most of them also had their final interview with the U.S. Consulate. Most of them passed and few were failed. I was very nervous. What about if I failed the interview? I had to ask everyone, I practiced all the questions the consulate may ask me. The night before my interview, I really prayed so hard and asked the Lord to help me to pass the interview. I wasn't sure how many hours I slept, but I was ready that morning. I arrived at the U.S. Embassy compound. I was standing on the other side of the hallway waiting for my number to be called. I was still very nervous and shaking, suddenly they called my number to report to window #3. I walked slowly, I finally reached the window, and the U.S. Consul was a young man probably around 26 years old. He was staring at me. He made me very uncomfortable. He had all my files and started to examine. Each time he flipped the page, he would look at me eye to eye. I just smiled but I was shaking all the way to my bones. My heart was beating so fast. He knew I was very nervous. It had been almost twenty minutes. The consul had never asked me one question. I asked myself, "What is happening?" And he kept on reading all the documents all the way to the last one. I saw him stamped the last page, and signed it. He kept on staring at me again and again. Why couldn't he ask me questions??? "Why, Why?!!!! Finally, after he finished examining all the documents, he gave me a piece of paper and said, "Here are the instructions for you to follow to have your physical in our U.S. hospital. Make sure to return again to the Embassy once your result from the hospital is completed". Then I said, "Sir, there's no more interview?" He replied, "Young man, get out of here, there's no more interview, good luck to you." He smiled at me before I turned around to exit. I smiled back and told him thanks. I turned back one more time, he was still smiling and he waved his hand, goodbye. I was so excited but I didn't understand why I didn't get the interview, I was ready and prepared to answer. Did he feel sorry for me? Or what kind of impression I gave to him? So far, I was the only person who was so lucky not having the interview. Every single person had their moment, but still it puzzled me. I did not know anyone at the U.S. Embassy. My prayers were answered, and I thanked God once again.

Chapter 15

After two days I went to the U.S. hospital. Instead of giving me an X-ray, I had this tuberculosis test on my left arm. The nurse told me once the injection turned red, I would be required for an X-ray to my chest. Unfortunately, the T.B Test turned red the shape of a dime. I showed my friends, they all scared me to death. They all told me I had Tuberculosis. I was so worried. "What happens if I am sick?" I didn't sleep that night. I knew I had to go back to the hospital the next day. Since my TB test was red, I needed an X-ray. I had it done that day. It would take another 3 or 4 days to find out the result. Again, I needed to pray harder this time, because this was the final test. I saw dark clouds in the sky. I needed the sunshine to brighten my day. When the hospital found out I was sick, then it would be the end of everything. My future would stop there. I felt it was the end. It was again, one more sleepless night. "Tomorrow I have to find out the result of my chest X-ray". I was not excited going there anymore. I wanted to turn around to go home and forget everything. But I changed my mind. I needed to find out the result no matter what. If I was sick, then I had to face reality. But it would be a big shame and I would not able to face anybody, especially all my friends. I went straight to the counter. They told me to proceed to the next door to my right. There they would give me the result of my X-ray. Suddenly, I saw the nurse holding a very large brown envelope. "Are you Mr. Mulinyawe?" I nodded, meaning yes. I was just so nervous. She said, "Here's the result of your X-ray, make sure you surrender this to the Immigration in Hawaii" I said, "You mean my test was negative?" She replied, "Yes, you're fine". Again she had to remind me that I needed to take my results to the U.S .Embassy. I almost forgot about it. I felt my body was floating up in the air. I almost cried but I held it in. "Mission accomplished.... I am really going to Hawaii". I didn't stop talking to myself and at the same time I kept on saying, "Thank you God" over and over again. It was the best moment of my life really!!! I could not believe everything turned out well. The way I planned and the way things had worked out. I just could not believe it.

The following day I went to the US embassy with my head up high. I took my time, at that moment I had no fears, no sadness but very happy, indeed. I went to pay the fee and I got my visa, I still couldn't believe it. The same day I purchased my one way plane ticket to Hawaii. I called Elder Parkinson at the mission home, he was so happy for me for all the things I had accomplished. I proudly said, without him and GOD I could had not done it. I was so thankful for all the good examples I had received from my friend, Elder Parkinson. I did not think I would find time to see him, because I was leaving in three days, but I told him he must stop in Hawaii after he was released from his mission, and I promised to show him around.

I took the bus home to my boarding house. All of my papers and everything were in one big envelope. The next day I went to work. I had to tell my supervisor the good and the bad news. I didn't know where to start. First the bad news, "Sir, I will be quitting my job this week. I am so sorry to give you a short notice. But I must resign". My boss was surprised and asked me, "Why young man? Why are you quitting your job?" Then the good news, "Well, I will be going to Hawaii to attend college there," He said, "How on earth did this happen? How come you never told us about it?" I said," Well, I wasn't really sure but here are the proofs". I showed him my passport, my visa and my plane ticket as well. Upon seeing everything, he said to me, "Wow, you are really leaving us! I am very happy for you, you are such a nice guy and you worked really hard. Please send us a card from Hawaii." I thanked my boss for the opportunity he had given me and all the kindness everyone showed me. I knew it would be a hard goodbye to all but, I had to go. I would surely miss them. When I got back to my apartment, I talked to my landlord about me not staying longer so I needed to know how much I owed for the rent and the meals. Everyone was surprised and few of them were kind of jealous. I told them I would send a post card from Hawaii. Romy, my roommate, he was very happy for me. I would miss him as well.

Chapter 16

The next day, I had to make my final trip home. I had my new suitcase full of new clothes. Some members had my clothes tailored. One family bought me new shoes, I also had some extra money from them. It was so nice of them to care about me. I really did appreciate everything they had done. I was blessed with so many good people that were looking after me, I could not possibly ask for more. I took a taxi cab all the way to the bus station, it would be an hour and a half before I reached my home town. I was thinking and thinking about my life. It would be very interesting to face those people in my town. Most of them used to look down on me before. I wonder what would be their reaction now. I always felt I didn't belong there, where I was born. But now, it would be so much different. I had something to be proud of, especially my dear mother. I finally arrived, I was walking on the street carrying my new suitcase. No one asked me why, but I just gave them my warmed smile. I knew that day rumors would spread right away. They would be wondering what was going on, why I came home with my big suitcase. My mother saw me coming yards away, and she was surprised upon my arrival. At first, I needed a glass of water before I started talking. I didn't see my stepdad just my mom. Then I said, " Mom, I have something to tell you, please do not tell anybody because no one will ever believe you. In three days I'll be leaving for Hawaii to attend college there." My mom suddenly replied, "Son, how did it happen? We are so poor, I didn't have money to help you please tell me how you did it?" I said, "Mom, it is a very long story, but please keep quiet and do not tell anyone, promise me". Well, my mother was so overwhelmed and her excitement really made her so proud of me. She didn't listen to me, she then told everyone in the village, and the rumors started. It was a big gossip item. What I heard was, my mom was crazy telling everybody her son was going to study in Hawaii and yet they were poor as rats. I didn't get mad at my mother, I didn't blame her at all, and I knew she was just so happy for me. Most people said I would be back in a week or two because my visa was not real, it was fake, and that's what everyone was saying. Some people came to congratulate me but still had their doubts. I really never paid attention to the critics, all I knew was this was really the part of my long journey. First and foremost, I knew everything was real and that I was ready to go abroad. I also asked myself, "How on earth did it happen?" I would find the answers sooner or later.

Chapter 17

The day came, I rented a jeep for my family to see me off. I saw people in my town lining on the street, my grandpa and my grandma were there as well. I didn't know it was the last time I would see them, "Bless their souls". I waved goodbye to them but no one ever said anything they were just staring at me. I wasn't sure if they were wishing me the best or what? All their arms were tight on their chests, "Why couldn't they say goodbye?" Should they be proud of me? Well, I just said, "See you all in a week or two." We left very early because we did not want to get stuck with the heavy traffic. I was hoping the weather would cooperate, when there was rain it would take us forever before we reached the airport. We had a long way still, inside the jeep we were all so quiet. My sister and my mother looked very sad. Along the highway I asked our driver if he could stop to buy some fresh drinks for everyone. We stopped for a while, I started to feel sad. I am going to miss everyone so, what about my own country? We arrived in the airport around 12 noon. There I met one of my friends who worked there. To my surprise he took me and my family to the VIP room. Only dignitaries and high class people were allowed there but somehow we all got in there until my departure. I saw those rich people, compared to us there was a big gap. But I was so thankful to my friend for what he had done for us. After an hour or two, I had to say my final goodbye. I embraced my mom once again, then my sister, and then the rest of my family and few friends who came along. It was sad, lots of tears here and there. I didn't cry that much, I had to wait until I got on the plane. I and my two companions went straight to the boarding gate. They were also new student to attend

BYU-Hawaii. It was so strange the way I was feeling. I wanted to cry already but I controlled it. I realized the final step towards the door of the plane, I quickly turned around to wave goodbye, I knew my folks were there at the window of the VIP room, watching me until my plane was ready to take off. I got into my seat, buckled my seatbelt, it was my very first time to ride the plane so I was very nervous. The captain of the plane announced that we were ready to take off. The plane started running on the runway, it would be a few minutes or so before the plane was ready to fly. I sat nervously, I looked at the passenger next to me, and he was very relaxed. Then the plane finally took off, I guessed we were almost 30,000 feet high or more, I saw the clouds, left and right, most windows were opened. We were really over on top of the skies!!! The flight would be around eleven hours or less. What would I do during this time? I would never sleep, I wanted to be awake in case the plane crashed into the ocean. The hungry sharks would be there, waiting for me. After 4 hours, I had a nose bleed, my ears were clogged. I couldn't hear anything. The stewardess came to help me, I got better afterwards. Most passengers were sleeping. I wouldn't ever sleep. I started reading magazines available in the pocket of the plane seat. The guy next to me woke up, I introduced myself to him. His name was August. He told me he was going to be an exchange student. His final destination would be Washington. I knew he still had a long flight before then. He told me his dad was working for the Philippine government. He told me he was attending at the Ateneo University in Manila. That school was mostly for rich boys. I knew August belonged to a wealthy family the way he dressed and the way he looked. But he never at one time intimidated me, he was so polite and very respectful. I wished him the best.

Chapter 18

We still had four more hours before the final destination. I tried to close my eyes maybe I would fall asleep. I knew I was on the plane, in the sky flying. Was this for real? Am I only dreaming? If I am, I didn't want to wake up. I really fell asleep for a while because the cockpit made an announcement that we would be landing in about one more hour. I felt the plane was going down. The plane was shaking a little bit. I remembered someone told me before, that the danger for any plane was taking off and touching down. I felt we were ready for touch down. The plane slowly landed, the pilot did a good job, and we were all safe and sound. I heard the announcement, WELCOME TO HAWAII!! I was so relieved, no more worries. I felt very good. The plane was completely stopped and we were now at the gate to the US Immigration Service. We started getting out, formed the line to be inspected by the Immigration officer. My two other companions were behind me. We had to be prepared to show our passport, visa and the x-ray result. I was holding it very carefully. I still saw lots of people ahead of us so we had to be patient. I looked around, lots and lots of people there. I needed to see out the window a little bit of Hawaii. I was anxious to get out, that way I wanted to make sure I was already on the island. We just got it through, there were no problems about our documents. The officer said, "Welcome to Hawaii, enjoy your stay". Outside the terminal three of us met the Dean of students who would take us to the BYU-HAWAII campus. He had a very big car, I was sitting way in the back. I was talking to myself silently. "Wow", I am really here, in Hawaii." We took the road were we could see the ocean and blue skies. I enjoyed the trip everything was beautiful, the mountains were all green, coconut trees everywhere. Different wild flowers along the roads, it was breath taking. We arrived on Campus, I was headed to the men's dormitory. I said, "God, I felt like a rich kid", going to attend college and now I am here at my dormitory. How? I meant to say how could it happen? I didn't care if I was tired but the dorm parents told us we needed to rest because of the jetlag. I was told tomorrow was our orientation, touring around campus and meeting new students from different parts of the world.

Chapter 19

The next morning I couldn't get up. I was so tired. I needed to attend the orientation. I dressed up, but I forgot, I needed to shower first. Then later, I went to the auditorium where all new students gathered. I saw all my friends, they arrived in Hawaii earlier. I guessed I and my two companions were the last to arrive. I heard there were 60 Filipinos that made it. I didn't know most of them, some came from the other parts of the Philippines. We were all happy meeting each other. That day was Friday, the whole day, we were able to complete the orientation. All the school loans for the semesters were offered to us, including for the dormitory and board. We were given books and school supplies. We had to sign an agreement that we all have to obey the rules and regulations of the school. We have to maintain our grades and make sure to take twelve credits or more each semester. If we failed in school we would be subjected to report to the Immigration. Each of us had to be assigned in different dormitories. The school had three buildings for women and three buildings for men. I was assigned in men's dorm two. The next day was Saturday, they provided us the school bus to go down town Honolulu. The driver first took us to Waikiki Beach, I heard that name back in the Philippines in one of the movies I saw. I could not imagine that I would be able to walk along the famous beach, everyone was having a good time. The waves were coming down the shore, surfers riding against the waves. I am really here in the beautiful island.

We spent the whole day in downtown Honolulu. We went to see the International Market in the heart of downtown. I saw something that I wanted to buy, but I changed my mind, I did not want to spend my little money in my wallet. There would be lots of time to come for shopping. It was time for us to go back to BYU-Campus. There were still a few more guys that the driver was waiting for. If they did not show up on time to leave, then they would be stuck in town. Luckily, they were back just in time. It was already dinner time when we all arrived on campus. We went straight to the school cafeteria. Each of us had to show our I.D. and we could have our meals.

The cafeteria was big. It could handle five hundred students and the place was packed. I was already in line when I saw my friends already eating on the other table. I got a tray and the girl served my food. There were so many different kinds of food, I didn't know what to choose. I said to myself, "From now on I will eat a lot, and drink milk for my bones, that way I could grow taller." We had so many good discussions, everyone was excited. I was a little quiet, I still could not believe what was happening to me. "From the beginning, I was very poor and struggling but now, I am here."!! I still had so many unanswered questions that were accumulating into my brains...I would have to sort things out in many days to come.

That night we celebrated our first Saturday night's dance, there was a live band. I was so amazed, the music was fantastic. The band was playing Carlos Santana, (Magic Woman) and a girl came to me and asked if I wanted to dance. I couldn't say no, she was so beautiful and a good dancer. That was my first time to meet any Hawaiian girl, we danced for about four songs. I saw those Filipino guys really having such a good time as well. We were outnumbered, they were more girls than guys that night, so I took advantage dancing with different girls. It was my very first time in my life to have that experience, I felt like I was on top of the world. I saw lots of Polynesian people from Tahiti, Samoa, Tonga and New Zealand, there were also those native Hawaiians. Again, I just couldn't believe how happy I was, being with so many different people from different parts of the world. I could never imagined that moment in time, it was so much fun. I did not want to end it.

The following Monday, I went to register and picked all my classes, I wanted to focus on the requirements first, and maybe the next semester I would take some major classes. At midday, I went to the employment office. I needed a part time job to support my expenses. I was told that the school was required to withhold my earnings every week to credit into my loan for the fall and spring semesters, and then I would receive $10 allowance every month. Also I was told, every summer I had to work two jobs in order for me to earn enough money to pay the school. By doing that, it would be easier to get a new loan. It was a hard time for me to get by with $10 allowance every month, but I was able to budget it, like buying detergent soap for the laundry, toothpaste, body soap, etc. I made sure I had few dollars left, so when we to go to Honolulu on weekends, I could buy my good lunch at the Chinese place, by then it would cost only one dollar per plate. They gave us a lot and sometime I could not finish it. I did mostly window shopping, when I had a chance to save money, then I could buy little things that I liked.

Chapter 20

It was already summer, we had to go to Honolulu to look for full time jobs. I was lucky to find one at the restaurant as a bus boy, then one at the nearby hotel as a janitor. Total of sixteen hours a day for both jobs. I shared a room with eight guys, we all split equally for the apartment rent. I stayed at my job for less than three months. I had all my pay checks with me ready to give the school. I did not have a chance, to send money to my mother, I was sure she was waiting for it. I would have to explain to her my situation, and maybe I could find a way somehow, to send her money.

Everything went well, I have to be ready for the Fall Semester. I was able to clear my old loan, then I had to apply for the new loan for another two semesters. It was like repeating the same old routine. Oh, let me mention about my seven roommates. Our room had eight beds, with wood partitions, in front of each bed was just a curtain, there was only one entrance door. I had to make sure when I fall sleep, the curtain must be closed. That was the only privacy we all had. My roommates were, two Chinese, one Samoan, one Tongan, one Tahitian, one Japanese, and two Filipinos including myself. My Japanese roommate was very funny, his name was Kazuo Kazuga. He had terrible problem pronouncing letter L, in Japan their alphabet did not have that letter L. I introduced him to my Filipina friend, and they both fell in love with each other. One night Kazu came home, he was telling me about her new girlfriend Sonia. I said to Kazu, "What did you tell her in English, Kazu?" Then he said, "Sonia, I rerry rrobe you." Then I said to him, "Kazu you have to say I really love you, not I rerry rrrobe you." Kazu never really learned to pronounce those letters. He had a guitar, and you could imagine when he tried to sing the song, titled, Leaving on the Jet Plane! There were lots of rrrreeeeving and prrrrrrrain, but he was a very cool guy, and well behaved. My Tahitian friend's name was Gerard Yao. He was 90% Chinese but he was born in Bora Bora, and he spoke French. I was always blessed to meet nice people. One time Gerard asked me about my mom, I said, she suffered too much with my stepdad and she also had a grown goiter hanging on her neck. He felt bad for her when I showed him my mom's photo. That next week it was his payday. We went to a little private room, and he wanted to talk to me. I was thinking why he needed to talk to me. He told me, "Listen my friend, I want to help your mother, and I will pay for the cost of the operation for your mom to remove the goiter over her neck. I was speechless. I replied and I said, "Gerard, I don't think I can accept your offer, for the reason, you worked so hard and you will just give away your money, just like that." Then he said, "Come on, I know you cannot afford to help your mom at this time. Then, let me do it for you and your mother especially, I will be offended if you refused my offer." I was surprised because it was so nice of Gerard to do that. I thanked him, and we became good friends. After a month, my mother was operated on with the helped of Gerard. He paid a lot of money for my mom's surgery. Gerard worked in the kitchen of the Polynesian Cultural Center, he was already a supervisor there, and he was in charged of the food department. He specialized carving fresh pineapples, he would carve each one and put sherbet ice cream on top. The girls dressed with their long MUMU, and flowers in their hair, would be serving the delights to the tourists during one hour intermission. The show at the center was really spectacular. I knew most of the dancers there. Most of them were students as well. It was a great program of the University helping those kids from different islands in the Pacific, to work and go to school at the same time.

By the way, Elder Parkinson stopped by the Polynesian Cultural Center accompanied by three other Elders, four of them were released from their missions simultaneously. When they were at the center I purchased their tickets for the show, and I made sure my friend Gerard made special pineapple delights. He picked the biggest pineapples and made four of them. When I saw the Hawaiian girl approaching the Elders to deliver the pineapple delights, most people on the bench were outraged, upon seeing those big pineapples. They enjoyed the show very much. The next day, I skipped school and I toured them around the island. I guessed, they were all happy for what I had done for them. The following day I had to do another goodbye. I could not count how many of those I made during the past years, my friend Richard was so happy for me, and he was proud for everything I had done for myself. He would be lookig forward to see me in the mainland in the near future to

Chapter 21

I hit my junior year in college and I became more productive. I felt like I made so many accomplishments though I still have another year and a half to go. I got a new job at the Polynesian Cultural Center. My first position was to collect money from all the cash registers in many different departments. The most money I collected was from the gift shops and the food court as well. That year there were so many Japanese tourists, for them money was nothing, sometimes they were having a hard time counting the dollars, especially $100 bills, but most of us at the center were very honest and we never took advantage of any tourist. We spend so much time counting all those cash dollars, if I was short like a quarter, and I had to get it from my own pocket. We made sure we were all balanced when we finished the reports. Our supervisor was so grateful for our efforts and dedications to our jobs. I did not stay long in that department. I was moved to do payroll, and I handled all time cards of the staff and the dancers that worked at the center. I really liked my job because it helped me a lot to pay for my schooling. My boss told me I could work more hours like Saturdays. There was the Laniloa Lodge next to the center. It was a privately owned business. The lodge provided good lunches and dinners for the tourists that arrived at the center, and I was able to work there like fifteen hours a week. I was doing the table and working at the kitchen. I felt guilty not telling the school about my employment at the Lodge, but I needed to send a little money to my mother every month. Anyway, my salary at the center went straight to the school to pay my current loan. So, everything went alright. I was lucky the

Lodge did not report me to the school. They really liked me there.

During my senior year, I joined the Showcase Hawaii. It was also sponsored by the University and Randy Booth was our musical director. We were 30 of us in the group. It was a wonderful opportunity for me because I loved music so much. The director composed different varieties of music. I had a solo number and he was the one who played the piano for our all music background. He was superb. We rehearsed after school. Our group traveled in the island of Oahu to perform in some communities, hospitals and Detention Center. One time, we performed for the late President Kimball. It was my very first time to meet an Apostle. He was smiling and enjoying our musical presentations. I saw him clapping, he was really pleased the way we entertained Him. After the show, we came down to shake his hand. It was such a very spiritual moment, and meeting him face to face was one of my most unforgettable experiences.

The same year, I met a girl, (I cannot say her name) she was so sweet and a very loving woman. I thought we were just friends but she fell in love with me. I had never taken advantage of her. I made sure I respected her in many ways I could. One night, she was at the house of my friends at the marriage housing project of the University. She locked herself in the bathroom and tried to cut her wrist. I was terribly scared as I did not want any bad thing happened to her. Thank goodness she was okay. After two weeks, I tried to talk to her to convince her that our relationship was just friends. She was so understanding at that time, and I was happy about it. I controlled myself by not seeing her but I really felt bad.

It was very hard for me to study and work, but I was nearly in my senior year. I could not believe it, although I was not an A's student I was able to fulfill to pass every subjects I took and to the very end of my college year. I had never failed any of my major subjects, if I got C's or B's it would be heaven for me, and I have to celebrate.

I only made an A on my Psychology class and that was it....at least I was not that dumb after all. I always remember the motto I learned from my friend Richard, "IF YOU FAIL TO PREPARE, PREPARE TO FAIL." So, I did all that, I supposed there were no regrets!!!

Chapter 22

Now, I was about to graduate, I checked the office to make sure I had all the requirements they needed for me to qualify to march for the coming graduation ceremony, then they told me I had completed everything and there was no problem at all. I ordered my cap and gown, I was very excited. It was not real for me that this was happening. Two days before the graduation, I got a message to report to the office of the education department. I said, "Now what!!! Don't tell me there is something wrong?" Well, there was …..I was told that I would not be able to march because I was lacking one required subject that I thought I did not have to take. When I saw them the first time, they told me I was okay and then suddenly, I was told that I was not. After all the excitement? It was very cruel of them to not to let me march. I begged them but they could not break the rules. I needed to take the math class which I hated it so much. When I was in grade school I was good in math but when I went to college, my brains gave up. After two days I was sobbing in my dorm, I wanted to be with those guys I went to school with, and to experience walking on the stage receiving my diploma. But it did not happen. Same day, I asked a friend of mine to come to the dorm to take my pictures with my cap and gown. They turned out very well. I sent some pictures to my family, but I never told them what had happened.

In two weeks, I took the math class and I got a C... better than F. but it still hurt me so bad. They told me I could march for the next graduation year and to let them know where I was, they would send me the formal invitation to march. They did, but I was not interested anymore. I felt I did not finish college even though I got my diploma. I even sent my mother the original copy but it was stolen in the mail. Someone benefited from it after all those years of hard work and endurances. Even up to the end I had to suffer. Life had never been perfect for me.

After all those agonizing experiences, I realized that everything was part of God's plan on how I would endure to the end. I cannot have everything in life, but I must accept all the trials and tribulations that was given to me. I became a much better person and developed a very strong faith in GOD.

FINAL CHAPTER

I couldn't ask for anything else. For all the people that I have met from the beginning of my journey, I have to admit how lucky I was. First, I have to thank God. HE helped me so much and blessed me to meet those wonderful people who guided me in the past. The family in Los Banos, their son Resty, my friend Rick at the radio station, the Abao's, the members of my two wards, the people in the office in Manila, the Broadbent family, the Pambids, the consulate at the U.S. Embassy, my Tahitian friend Gerard, Kazu Kazuga from Japan, everyone I met at the University, my family especially my mother, my sister Andrea, my stepdad who died and before his final breath he told my mom, "Tell my son I am sorry.", It was a little too late but I have forgiven him, the Elders, and most importantly, my brother Richard. I appreciate all the love and care he showed me and his beautiful and loving wife Marla. They now have 29 grandchildren. Without God and Richard, my life probably would have turned upside down. The Gospel was the main key for my success. Every single soul I mentioned in my life story was part of the long, long journey I took. I chose the right road and I never looked back. Everything that the Father in Heaven said to me, really happened. But you all know how I went through and how I endured. It was not easy, but I did not give up and I continued what I had to do. Now, I found out all the unanswered questions I have been waiting for a long time.

I have learned so much since my life story began. Wealth is not everything in life but FAITH matters the most. God wants us to love one another, HE SAID, LOVE EACH OTHER AS I HAVE LOVED YOU, it doesn't matter the color of our skin, or where we came from, and we still breathe the same air. We are all children of God, we should respect each other, and we should always be ready to face our Father in Heaven and his Son Jesus Christ. I was there once, it was really beautiful, and now I am not afraid to die. We must always accept the Gospel and set a good example to others. I am ready anytime God wants me. He is watching us every single moment. We have to be prepared when our time comes. Every one of us has our own destiny, we all have different stories to tell, to write, and to share with our families and friends. I do hope I convey a message to everyone. No matter who and what we are, everything is possible if we have strong faith. I thank you all so dearly for reading my book. I will do my very best to be perfect, I know it is not that easy, but all of us must try. By obeying God and accepting the Gospel, I can go to Heaven once again, to face our Father and His son Jesus Christ at "HEAVEN'S DOOR."

CPSIA information can be obtained
at www.ICGtesting.com
Printed in the USA
FSOW04n1716021116
26901FS